RECONNECTING WITH YOUR KIDS

DEDICATION

This book is dedicated to those hard-working, harried, doing-their-best parents who feel they are losing the battle to hold their families together in the midst of their busy world, watching as their children spin away from them.

It is also dedicated to the children who have come and gone from my home. Thank you for the lessons you taught me as I tried my best to parent you. How wonderful that God took over and changed everything.

Thank you for the Little People Stories you all gave me to lighten my day. For instance, stories like this one:

As I talked to a little girl on Face Time I said, "I'm sorry you're sad Beighley. I can see you are crying. Are you going to be okay so we can talk?"

Sniffling and wiping tears from her eyes, she said, "Yes, but my eyes is still melting."

RECONNECTING WITH YOUR KIDS

How to Restore Relationships in Three Fun, Free, Easy Steps

CONTENTS

CHAPTER ONE:
THE REVELATION, COURTESY OF A REAR-VIEW MIRROR

As a family with two employed adults, we needed two cars but only had one. After much prayer, someone gave us an automobile. I use the word automobile instead of car because it conjures up images of long, low, lumbering vehicles as wide as two modern day cars with oversized steering wheels. You've seen them in movies about the mob in Chicago. It was that kind of vehicle. It was an AUTOMOBILE, if you get my drift. We were grateful for this gift and the freedom it gave us. We fought daily over this car, my husband and I. Neither one of us wanted to drive it. It was a bit like driving a tank. I am short and had to peer over the steering wheel to drive. The one thing about that car that challenged me most was that rear-view mirror.

It seemed to be fine on long stretches of road, but the minute I applied the brake, all kinds of things started to happen. The rear-view mirror would suddenly leave its position and swoosh downward so I was only seeing the dashboard in it. It would sway there a few minutes until the light turned green, then it would fly up so I got a quick glimpse of the car's roof and would then lock back into place until the next red light. It needed constant attention. At some point, it dawned on me that the rear-view mirror in the AUTOMOBILE was getting more input from me than my own children got on any given day. The concern that I wasn't a very good parent reared its ugly head. Again.

Around that time in our lives, I had a conversation with my preschool daughter that went like this:

Holly: I saw an amblanx today.

Me: That must have been exciting.

Holly: It was loud and went fast. I want to be an "amblanx" person when I grow up.

Me: I think you can be whatever you want to be when you grow up.

I debated with correcting her pronunciation of ambulance because I thought it was cute. So, I let it go.

Then my son, 4 years older than she, and an avid reader, had a conversation about a shirt he wanted:

Aaron: I really like the "played" shirt, mom.

Me: Which one is that?

Aaron: This one (pointing to a plaid shirt in the catalog).

Me: It is very colorful. Maybe we can get that for you.

I debated with correcting his pronunciation of plaid but I thought it was cute. So, I let it go.

The guilt kept on stacking up as each child came to me later pretty upset. They told me they didn't think it was funny that I didn't correct them on their pronunciation of those words. Their classmates weren't as nice as I would have been. I apologized and decided to actually pay closer attention to their vocabulary development. It was another opportunity to feel guilty about my time investment in my children.

I wondered, "When had those kids learned those words?" It wasn't that long ago that Holly could only repeat the things that she heard us say around the house or the things she picked up at church. She had no other sources of information. I suspected that Aaron got his word "played" from the latest catalog he was reading. He pronounced it the way it was written.

I didn't like the fact that all the new things these kids were learning were coming from some source other than us. Home schooling, my preferred choice, was not possible since we both had to work. There was some comfort in the fact that I knew that their Christian elementary school would teach them many of the things I would have. However, I wanted to be a part of that process. There was simply no time.

I knew Aaron would read everything he got his hands on and outdistance my feeble attempts at making sure he only learned what I thought was good and right, which is probably as it should be. Holly would soon be caught up in the world of school activities and church youth trips and would grow farther away from us.

Was that really the way it was supposed to happen? Was there a way to let them go and yet still maintain the heart-closeness we had shared when they were younger? The real issue was that I missed my kids, even though we lived in the same house.

I felt I needed to seek answers and began to read anything available on parenting, working parents, school aged kids and ways to improve my organizational skills. Most suggested ideas that simply didn't fit our family. Elaborate plans for vacations or participating in sports together wouldn't work for us, partly because of finances, and partly because we no longer shared common interests. I began to pray about how I could be more of a presence in the lives of my kids. It became clear that many things had to change, starting with our routine.

See if you can identify your family in this scenario:

Alarm clocks go off and people rush from their rooms, heading for bathrooms, then back to their rooms to get dressed and make beds. "Mom! I can't find my backpack!" "Oh no, where is my other shoe? I need it for P.E. today." They trickle out to the kitchen for breakfast. At any given time, one or two members of the family are missing from the table when the others start eating. When the first shift is done, the others run into the kitchen. Rides to school come and go, cars leave the house and the cat or dog or iguana are left in silence. Later the front door flies open, kids scuffle for snacks, music from several radios blast through the house, homework is completed or not, paper bags open, fast food is tossed on the table and someone calls out that dinner is ready. After dinner kids go to their rooms with their electronics and adults steal a quiet hour with the television or Face Book.

When our kids were in elementary school, our lives were almost like that, except for the technology part. And the fast food part. Okay, sometimes the fast food part. Thankfully, I had this fascination with crock pots and felt compelled to put meals in the crock pot that were ready when we got home. Unfortunately, it was rare that any of us got home at the same time. My son worked after school at a baseball card shop, riding his bike there and back. My daughter was involved in elementary school activities at a school that had no busses. Someone picked her up every night after her activities. She was also very active in the youth group and had activities throughout the week.

My job as a victim advocate kept me at work very late most nights, meeting with crime victims or waiting for jury verdicts after long trials. My days also started very early. Sometimes I would just get home, get the mom chores done, and fall exhausted into bed when my pager would go off. As Division Chief of the County Attorney's Victim Witness Division, I had established a crisis response team to go to crime scenes with law enforcement. We were on call with several law enforcement agencies in the area and were called out when a victimization occurred. There were times when I was at crime scenes or the hospital all night with victims. When I was out past 7:00 am, the family would get up and get themselves off to school and work.

My husband's job sometimes required him to be home quite late. He was occasionally in another part of the county when it was time to pick someone up from school or a church activity. We really needed that second automobile, but it only added to our crazy, busy lives. Now we could go in entirely different directions without the need to sit in a car for a half hour and talk or listen to a child's story about what happened that day. Despite how well put together we appeared as a family to outsiders, the truth was that we were four people spinning in our own circles apart from each other. I pictured a bicycle tire with the center hub and spokes going out from the center. The spokes were only loosely connected to the center, which was where the stability was supposed to be. That was us, and it alarmed me.

Something had to change and I needed to be the catalyst to bring it about.

When I began praying about what to do, I ended up with several great ways to reconnect my family. We desperately needed to get to know each other again, other than during the unpleasant interactions fighting for the bathroom in the mornings. I didn't make a major announcement about all of them, because my great, new, fun family activities were often met with groans. I simply quietly worked them into our lives.

I am sharing with you the three most successful ideas. These have become my all-time favorites. The beauty of these activities is that they don't necessarily add another layer to your life. They are fun. They are free. Pick one or two or three to implement. Two of them take place at the family dinner table. Don't have a family dinner table? Make a point to connect at least once a day with your spouse and children over a meal. It is an investment well worth your time and effort. Actually, these ideas are easier than you might think. You just shift your focus to incorporate these ideas into what you are already doing.

Single parent? It was you whom I had in mind when I first thought about this book. There are very special demands on single parents that two-parent homes know nothing about. Because of that, some of these ideas work equally well for single parents and others are set up to work more smoothly with two-parent households. They can be modified to fit any family. Just choose the one or two that you can incorporate into your life without adding a layer of guilt because you don't do it every day. These aren't rules but are suggestions that you can try, discard or keep, depending on whether or not they work for you. They could help bring you closer to your children.

I apologize to people in other parts of the world who never refer to their children as "kids." To them, kids are goats. In America, it is common to refer to children as kids and be quite respectful.

Let's get started with something I call Little People Stories which I have gathered over eight years as a therapeutic foster parent. I have found myself amazed at the things that kids say. I recorded a number of these interchanges and will share them throughout this book. This exchange took place with a Little Person, who regularly exhibited a penchant for making things better:

> *Me: Would you please put this puzzle in this bag and seal it tightly to keep the pieces together?*
>
> *Little Person: Sure.*
>
> *Me Later: Wow, that bag sure is full for having one little puzzle in it.*
>
> *Little Person: That's because I put that puzzle in a bag with the pieces from another puzzle.*
>
> *Me: So let me get this straight. You mixed two 500-piece puzzles in one bag? Can you explain to me why that's a good idea?*
>
> *Little Person: (Proudly) Because now, two people can work on the puzzle at the same time!*

(Note from me: FREE to first caller: 1,000-piece puzzle. Practically new.)

Three simple ways to reconnect with your family had long-range effects I couldn't have anticipated. Strangely, they fall into alphabetical order which may make them easier to remember. If you don't remember the first one by the time you are on the third one, no problem. Nothing in this small book is intended to add guilt you may already be feeling.

CHAPTER TWO:
ALL FOR ONE

This is a suggestion that works for both younger and older children, but works best for families with more than one child. With or without a partner, choose one child each week who could be the "star." That one gets to say grace over meals, and if they are older, they get to sit in the front seat of the car that week. The star could choose a family movie to watch, and generally find, or be given, ways to shine during that week.

If that child had something important going on at school or church, the rest of us would commit to moving Heaven and earth to be there to be supportive. (We modified our original "Star for a Month" because it was hard on the other child, since it took forever for their turn to roll around. "Star for a Week" seemed much more manageable and generated less arguing.) On a less grand scale, the adults got to be the star on occasion too. Finally, we began to operate as a family unit.

From the first time we implemented that plan, things began to change just a little around the house. The kids seemed to bicker less. Some of the competition between them seemed to lessen, although there would always be competition between a brother four years older than his little sister. Even if it wasn't that child's week, when something came up that was important to either child, the All for One activity went into high gear.

For instance, when our daughter was in the third grade, she bravely put aside her fears and decided to volunteer to sing a solo at the Christmas concert. We could have gone to the concert and met the goal of All for One that week. Instead, when she had a rehearsal, I would take an early or late lunch, walk over from the courthouse where I worked across the street from their school, and attend the practices. I would encourage her about how well she did, even though she was a puddle of tears from fear and embarrassment over flubs she had made. If Dad couldn't make it, I would take the movie camera (one the size CBS would use back in the day) slung over my shoulder and tape the rehearsal. Later Dad and brother could see how she did as she explained where she was about to make a mistake. Somehow, that lessened the impact of the mistakes for her and allowed us to praise her good work. Her confidence grew so much that by the night of the performance, she could belt out the song with confidence.

It is interesting to me that the more we supported her decisions to take the stage and be brave, the more she liked it. I bought an old, out-of-tune piano for $100 that had been painted green. When it was delivered to the house, she was ecstatic. Because she was showing commitment to music, we enrolled her in piano lessons when the "lean years" had passed. Before long she was singing and composing music. As she grew, she entered competitions in high school and attended a couple national events where she performed, singing a solo and ultimately singing a duet with her future husband.

Today our daughter is a wife and mother and the director of the Sunday School Department at her large church. She is encouraging her children to be involved in music. My five-year-old granddaughter recently sang a solo at their church. I thought of how introverted and shy my daughter was when she first decided to sing that solo in third grade and am amazed at what God has done with her life.

She is graceful and composed in front of a crowd and has become a confident public speaker. The idea of All for One seemed to be a turning point for her. She could have chosen to become a nurse or a doctor or a fireman or a chef, and it would have been fine. I am sure that the All for One encouragement she received would have given her the courage to follow wherever God led her in her life.

On another occasion, our son Aaron had entered his art work in a competition at school. The art exhibit was on display at a dinner function planned purposefully to raise funds for the school once a year. Normally we avoided that event because stretching our budget farther with a monthly pledge didn't seem possible. We didn't feel that we could go eat a nice meal and then not pledge to the school. That is a good example of simply deciding to be All for One, whatever the cost, setting aside any discomfort and going.

We were able to see his art work, meet his friends, and also make a small pledge to the school by faith. I remember watching him that evening as he enjoyed his friends, knowing his family was interested in his efforts by attending his first art show. He pretended that we were embarrassing him; but, as I told him later, that was our job. We all came away from that evening feeling a little better about ourselves.

I recently attended another showing of his artwork. He is now an adult, and I was proud to be able to go to the gallery and see his work hung on the wall with other artist's work. Of course, his was the best. Moms have to say that kind of stuff, but I think I'm right on this one. He is a very talented artist, working in various media. I'd like to think some of his comfort in the art realm came from feeling like his work was important to his family. It could also have something to do with the fact that he has been drawing since he was three. In the first grade he asked me if he could be an artist when he grew up. I distinctly remember telling him that he could be whatever he wanted to be as long as he was able to support himself and his family while he did it. He got giddy when I said yes (remember, he was seven), hugged me, and ran off to draw another masterpiece.

That's when I realized his art meant a lot to him. When he was old enough, I enrolled him in free art classes at the college in the summer to encourage his talent. I was familiar with the art world because my father was a professional artist. He was extremely talented and tried for years to teach me to "see" parts of the whole and paint them. I never got that, much to his frustration. Along came our son, who seemed to get all my father's talent but in supercharged mode. He studied graphic design and communication in college and has indeed been able to support himself and his family with his talent in art.

Who knew that God would take our feeble efforts to be All for One and turn them into bright futures for our kids? That great idea of All for One probably didn't come from me in the first place. It probably was something God whispered to me to help us pull our splintered family back together. I am so grateful for God's intervention in our lives.

Is your family fractured, going in separate directions like mine was? This little exercise went a long way toward helping us get re-acquainted. Was it easy? Sometimes it was not. However, if there isn't a vision of how you want your family to function, you have nothing to reach for. The Bible says that without a vision, the people perish.

Proverbs 29:18: Where there is no vision, the people perish: but he that keepeth the law, happy is he. (KJV)

How? Make a plan. Identify a vision. Then pursue that vision. You will be able to find ways to support your kids that I never thought about as you think about their unique talents, likes and dislikes.

I thought this Little People Story from my days as a foster parent might fit at the end of the All for One chapter:

>*In Little People Land on the way to the bus stop with a child who was starting her week as the "Star:"*
>
>*Little Person: La la la la, humming a familiar tune.*
>
>*Me: What is that you are singing?*
>
>*Little Person, getting out of the van, breaking into song: "La la la, Wouldn't it be Loverly" from My Fair Lady.*
>
>*Me: Glad you liked that DVD I gave you last night.*
>
>*Little Person: Like it? I LOVE it.*

I watched as she sang and danced a ballroom number from the van to the bus, arms outstretched, facing the sunrise. The dew was on the country grasses, and the air was damp from a midnight rain. What a great start to the day! Being the Star for the Week made a big difference for her.

CHAPTER THREE:
BE ASSURED AND ASSURING

My foster children and I got into the van later than I had hoped, racing out of the driveway, headed to town, 16 miles away for a doctor's appointment for one of them and some other meetings for me.

On the open road I glanced in the rearview mirror to confirm that everyone had seat belts on. Locking eyes with the shortest Little Person in the back seat, I heard:

> *Little Person: Oooohhh. Eye shadow.*

> *Me: Yes. I put on eye shadow. Why?*

> *Little Person: Enthusiastically strumming an air guitar. Well...you look like a rock star! A cool rocker!*

Ugh! I am apparently on my way to several professional appointments looking like a rock star. It was going to be THAT kind of day I guess.

There are many voices that can whisper in our ears throughout the day. The saddest of all voices are those accusing us of being somehow inadequate or being absentee parents in our children's lives. We don't want to be anything but great parents raising great kids. Sometimes, in a stroke of pure joy, reality overtakes fantasy, and we see that our kids, foster kids or others we care for are actually doing well; and we are okay too. Then comes the critical voice questioning our parenting skills again.

With this exercise, the end result will be that you will become your kids' greatest fan, moving them forward to become who God wants them to be. However, in order to get there, you will need to see how great is your own value. You need to be able to believe in yourself with knowledge that comes from God, rather than your own authority, which you are constantly questioning. How do you make that happen?

The Bible is full of statements of how valuable you are. Sometimes we just don't believe them.

1 Peter 2:9 reminds you how valuable you are as a chosen one, chosen specifically to be a mirror image of God's love on earth. That sounds impossible because the image you believe you reflect is that of a harried, disorganized person

always in a rush. God doesn't see you that way and told you:

> **But ye are a chosen generation, a royal priesthood, an holy nation, a peculiar people; that ye should shew forth the praises of him who hath called you out of darkness into his marvelous light; (KJV)**

I like the way The Message Bible puts it:

> **But you are the ones chosen by God, chosen for the high calling of priestly work, chosen to be a holy people, God's instruments to do his work and speak out for him, to tell others of the night-and-day difference he made for you—from nothing to something, from rejected to accepted. (MSG)**

From nothing to something, from rejected to accepted. He does not reject you. Are you rejecting yourself as a man or woman chosen of God to show His love to others, particularly your family first? If so, start with you. You are so important to God that He sent His only Son Jesus to die for your sins so you could be saved from eternal death. He wants you in eternity with Him since He knew you before you were born. Jeremiah 1:5 says

> **Before I formed thee in the belly I knew thee; and before thou camest forth out of the womb I sanctified thee, and I ordained thee a prophet unto the nations. (KJV)**

Again, The Message Bible brings that thought home for me:

Before I shaped you in the womb, I knew all about you. Before you saw the light of day, I had holy plans for you... Jeremiah 1:5 (MSG)

If He knew all about Jeremiah before Jeremiah even saw the light of day, He also knew you then and knew of the great plans He had for you. You are valuable. You are capable. You are faithful. You are the person God sees, not the person you see in the mirror every day. Start to find those gems in the Bible that speak of your great worth and you will begin to see yourself differently. Look in the mirror and see beyond the condemnation you have given yourself as though it were a gift. Instead, see the man or woman God created before you were born, one who He loves with an everlasting love. You are priceless!

Practice those affirmations from this moment on and notice the heaviness of failure begin to lift off your mind. "I see me as God sees me, through Jesus, and I am priceless to Him. I am greatly loved by the lover of my soul." If you do this, you may notice a physical "lightness" as the weight of the world comes off your shoulders and moves over to His.

Brace yourself though. About the time you get good at this, along comes someone to knock the wind out of you, such as the one in my next Little People story:

> *Little Person at the dinner table: You know what I miss?*
>
> *Me: No. What?*
>
> *Little Person: I miss the conversations at the table at my friend's house. Her whole family is really intelligent. Everyone was interesting. I miss that.*

Sigh. I don't believe I've ever had my conversational skills discounted so thoroughly. Thanks, Little Person. I may not be your conversational cup of tea, but I am chosen and favored by God, and that makes all the difference. That is how you re-frame any negativity that comes your way. I have to tell you that as I wrote this chapter, I came under a large shadow of depression. I questioned why I should be telling anyone else to value themselves when I saw little value in me. That is how the enemy works. I re-read the first part of this chapter a couple times and prayed for clarity of mind, and the depression lifted. It may not be easy to encourage yourself every day, but it is well worth it. You can do this. I believe in you.

Now for becoming your kids' biggest fan. You don't need to attend every sporting event or performance to show your kids that you love them. You can attend those you are able to attend, but when you can't, be their cheerleader anyway.

Having raised my own two children, done therapeutic foster care for eight years with 13 full time children and now having adopted a little girl, I have learned a few things. Kids sometimes act as though you are a bug on the wall, and they aren't the slightest bit interested in anything you say. However, when you are saying things like, "That was awesome how you helped that woman in the grocery store reach that box she couldn't. That made me proud of you even more" they hear you. This isn't the time to move in for a mom hug, but simply state your thoughts and continue with whatever you were doing. Your child's response may be a grunt or total silence, but that child has heard you. That is the type of message that goes into the ears, rattles around the brain for a minute and drops directly into the heart. That is an encouraging message, and it never fails to put some love glue into the tiny cracks that develop in a child's heart as they are navigating through life.

As my own children were growing up, we had several conversations about how faithful they were to do their chores. Someone would take out the garbage and announce to me that the garbage was out, waiting for a thank you. I used to be of the mindset that if you were simply doing what was expected of you, you didn't need accolades. Then I realized I was viewing this issue in the wrong way. I was passing up an opportunity to encourage my child by not acknowledging their commitment to the chore, not the chore itself. A simple thank you would have sufficed, but saying that I have noticed how diligent he or she is to do their chores or homework without being constantly prodded would have gone a long way.

I do not believe that every child who accomplishes something should have a ticker-tape parade. If Johnny who didn't put forth much effort, coming in 5th in the race, received the same prize as Philip, who came in first, where is the incentive for Johnny to improve next time? And where is the incentive for Philip to continue to strive for greatness? Rewarding children for showing up rather than reaching a goal robs them of the desire to improve. The same thing applies to children carrying out expected tasks. There is usually room to improve or go above and beyond with a task. Notice those mundane things and think of ways to frame your words to encourage your child.

I do, however, believe strongly in telling a child that they did a good job and really tried hard to win the race, adding "Next time I believe you can run even faster to the finish line. I am proud of you, son (or daughter)."

When I was working with foster children, I frequently gave prizes or extra privileges to them as they successfully completed a task or completed one without becoming frustrated and angry. Rewarding improvements was the key which helped them change their behaviors and actually try to make better choices to move closer to their "forever lives." Be generous with your praise and look for ways to let your children know their good deeds are being noticed and appreciated. It is likely that out in the world, classrooms and playing fields, they aren't being encouraged with kindness. Your home can be a place where kindness dwells and they can fill up on kind words so they can go out and face another day.

Life wasn't always picture perfect, even when I worked diligently at being assuring with my kids. When it came to arguments, and there were plenty of them, I learned a new skill which required me to think differently about conflict in my family. Basically, I began looking at the reasons and underlying feelings which gave rise to their behaviors, rather than the behaviors of arguing and emotional drama. I tended to get sucked into the drama and arguing, trying to settle every conflict that arose by acting just like the kids, sometimes worse. When I learned to understand reasons behind the feelings and the feelings behind the behaviors, I could address the root of behaviors and not just the surface evidence which I was seeing.

For instance, one of them would start an argument about not being able to go out on a school night with their friends. Instead of getting into that argument, I would think about his or her point of view, what it must feel like not to be able to join in the fun and feeling left out. I would address the feeling by saying, "I believe you are frustrated because your friends are out late on school nights, and our house rules don't allow for that except on rare occasions. I get that and want you to know when something special comes along, you will be able to stay out late. This just isn't the night." Approaching an argument from that angle often eliminated the argument completely. My children seemed to catch on to me because one evening my son said, "Mom, I don't know what you are doing, but you are freaking me out. So quit." They had noticed a difference in how I handled conflict, which I hope helped them think about their own problems in a different way.

As my children and foster children began to realize I was actually listening to them, we were able to move through conflict so quickly that most arguments never got off the ground.

There were the doozy-sized conflicts occasionally, which came with the territory when I began fostering. Early in my fostering career, it seemed that I had the most success with teen girls. If you have had teen girls in your home, you know that we had plenty of drama. We had shouting, door slamming, throwing things, and threats to run away. As I employed the plan to let each child know how valuable they were to God and to me, those episodes slowly became less frequent.

Being quick to compliment them on their improvements began to change how they saw themselves. One girl couldn't wait to get home after school and let me know she had only sworn four times that day. It was a personal best for her, and since it was an improvement, she was lavished with praise. Would I prefer that she didn't swear at all? Of course. Was I happy that she was working on improving? You bet.

The starting point is realizing that to God you are as valuable as a sparkling jewel. Your children are also valuable. You can convey that by watching for ways to praise them when they least expect it. They will think you are crazy when, out of the blue, you say, "I want you to know that I am really proud of you and I'm not just saying that because I'm your mom (or dad)." Maybe they will be caught off guard and actually give you a hug.

> *A Little People story that illustrates the difference in how we see ourselves and how others see us happened as I talked with one little guy:*
>
> *Little Person, talking very fast: And, you know, we went to Disneyland, and we rode on the fast rides...*
>
> *Me: Oh, that sounds fun.*
>
> *Little Person, not stopping to breathe: ...and we stayed in a hotel, and we ate fun food, and Mickey Mouse was there...*
>
> *Me: Did you get to talk to him:*
>
> *Little Person: ...and then we drove in the car for a long time, and I fell asleep, and we ate in a restaurant, and I love my mother, she's fat, and short, and beautiful, and she and dad got me fun stuff at Disneyland, and we get to go back, and when I go back I will go on the mountain ride, and...*

As he talked, I almost missed that zinger in the middle. I realized to kids, shapes and sizes are just part of a great story, worth mentioning, but not worth dwelling on. Too bad we can't be that kind to ourselves and each other.

CHAPTER FOUR:
CONNECT WITH ONE

This was another idea that helped congeal our family into more of a unit. This one involved matching a child with an adult to be responsible for dinner meals for a week. Because we had two adults and two children, this worked for us. It is possible to match two older kids with each other and have the parent matched with the younger one. A variation on this activity would be to have the kids prepare a part of the meal – a salad, or vegetables or dessert. There are no rules, so try whatever you believe might work. The fun is in team work.

The first week, Dad and son made the meals. They found out that this was not as simple as good old mom made it look. They managed to pull together some pretty impressive meals after quick thawing the meat which they forgot to take out of the freezer that morning.

The next week it was my daughter and me. Not to be outdone, she was in charge of the side dishes and desserts, and I made the main course. We were eating pretty well for the first part of this experiment.

The following week we switched, and it was mother/son on a team and father/daughter on a team. My daughter and I realized that there was precious little motivation with our new partners to make a cheap, hearty meal.

The third week of the month, it was mom/dad team and son/daughter team. I don't have much of a memory if that worked even one week, but I know I took over the cooking on the fourth week of the month. We were able to maintain this schedule almost one full summer.

The best plans can have unforeseen glitches in them and this was one. This time frame was also in the "lean times," as we call them. When you are going through difficult times, being creative with meals becomes something like doing a magic act. I remember the first night I knew this plan was going down the tubes. The father/son team had made dinner which consisted of cold cereal and popcorn. Okay, I thought, there are enough nutrients in cereal to make it marginally okay for a dinner meal. I presumed the popcorn was dessert. The following week, mother/daughter team did a little better with what could be found in the cupboards, but the choices were less and less appealing.

One evening is especially memorable. The kids entered the cake walk at one of the school's carnivals and won. Twice. That was a father/son night, and that was dinner. Not our best parental moment, but having cake for dinner felt like a party; and we were grateful to God for this provision. That's not to say we would have gone hungry. The Bible says:

> **Psalm 37:25: I have never seen the righteous forsaken nor his seed begging for bread (KJV).**

Slowly I resumed all the kitchen duties since I seemed to have the necessary wisdom to make something palatable by opening a can or a package, disguising it, and adding something green on the side.

The Connect with One plan didn't last forever, but it was fun and served to bring us together for a time. When we get together now, someone generally brings up that meal matching experiment and others chime in with memories. Making memories was a fun side effect of Connect with One.

It took no effort to implement this plan because we were going to be eating at some point in the evening. It also gave us something to talk about and kept conversation flowing. Invariably, someone dropped a major part of the meal on the floor and shared that little nugget of information only after we had eaten most of it. Or someone would say they forgot an ingredient (tough to do with cereal), and ask if it still tasted okay. We weren't solving the world's problems, but we were talking – actually talking. It felt good after many evenings of silence, or worse, arguing at the table.

God was doing an amazing thing for our family. We were becoming reacquainted with each other as people with hopes and dreams, friends and fears, and hearts slowing turning toward each other. God said that He would turn the fathers' hearts toward the children and the children's hearts to the fathers.

> **Malachi 4:6: And he shall turn the heart of the fathers to the children, and the heart of the children to their fathers...(KJV).**

This seemed to be an example of that gift played out before our eyes. If you are wondering how this can be fun, understand that if you believe every meal has to be perfect, with the basic 4 food groups on each plate, and that you will have some kind of control over how the meals appear on the table, you will not be having fun. Let go of the need to make the meals fit your mold and experience the fun of the journey through Connect with One.

Here is a Little People Story that illustrates communication in progress:

> *Little Person: Do I have to do my chores today before I watch a movie?*
>
> *Me: Yes, you need to get your chores done.*
>
> *Little Person: But I can do them after the movie.*
>
> *Me: They are to be done first. It's not negotiable.*

Little Person: What's negotiable mean?

Me: It means I'm not going to discuss it.

Little Person: But you are.

Me, looking her in the eye and smiling: I'm trying to be polite.

Little Person: If you were polite, you would let me watch a movie first.

And so it begins: Spirited discussions that will persist until my brain is tired and she nods off to sleep tonight. Guess which happens first.

At least we are communicating.

CHAPTER FIVE:
YOU CAN DO THIS

You can do any of these activities and stay at them until you see results. When you do, you may feel a change before you actually see it. For instance, you may sense a spirit of comradery before actually seeing it manifest. You may notice a kind word or a helping hand between your children that surprises you.

God can do anything in and through willing vessels. You have recognized that you are precious and valuable to Him. You have passed along that sense of value to your family who then can share it with each other and their friends. Small deliberate acts, consistently practiced will bring results. Mixing those acts with a healthy helping of fun creates memories.

You can make a difference in the lives of your children by investing in them in small ways such as those you have learned here.

God surely believes in you, and I believe in you! You can do this!

ABOUT THE AUTHOR

Claudia Thomason is an award-winning author of five books, including Kindergarten Lessons I Learned in Africa, Five Fun Animal Adventures from Africa, You Can Be Debt Free and Reconnecting with Your Kids. She is a Certified Parent Coach, Public Speaker and CEO of ReconnectingWithYourKids.com.

She has parented 13 children as a Therapeutic Foster Parent, raised two biological children – who now have families of their own – and recently adopted an 8-year-old girl with her own miracle story to share. Claudia has worked with children in Africa as an ordained pastor and continues to oversee a program there matching kids with sponsors for school fees and supplies.

This book is a result of discovering and implementing ideas to pull her family back together as they seemed to be gradually moving away from each other

Claudia has dedicated her life to helping children get through difficult times. She worked nearly 20 years in the criminal justice system with a focus on easing the suffering of children caught up in it. She trained judicial and law enforcement officials on victims' rights and received recognition from the Institutes for Law and Justice for her work co-creating a task force on domestic violence, recommending it as a prototype for other cities in the nation.

Claudia's passion is to see children raised in homes where they feel loved, valued and connected. She created Reconnecting with Your Kids to help parents find simple, fun ways to help their children. This results in families who have an increased ability to stay connected through life's ups and downs.

One of those ways: to find the joy in everyday moments, such as those contained in this book.

www.ingramcontent.com/pod-product-compliance
Lightning Source LLC
LaVergne TN
LVHW010024070426
835508LV00001B/36